I Can Talk about What Hurts

A Book for Kids in Homes Where There's Chemical Dependency

Janet Sinberg   Dennis Daley

Illustrated by Tim Hartman

HAZELDEN®

First published October 1989.

ISBN: 0-89486-641-9

Printed in the United States of America.

Editor's Note:
  Hazelden Educational Materials offers a variety of information
on chemical dependency and related areas. Our publications do not
necessarily represent Hazelden or its programs, nor do they officially
speak for any Twelve Step organization.

PREFACE FOR PARENTS

Addiction to alcohol or other drugs often has profound effects on other members of the family besides the addicted person.

Some recovery programs focus only on the addict while others bring family members into the treatment process. Whatever the model, we strongly believe that when there are children, they need the opportunity to come to terms with their parents' addiction and the impact it has had on their lives. This happens when they can get their problems out in the open and deal with them honestly.

Often, children don't have words to express what they are thinking or feeling. Many of them are afraid to talk about painful issues or events that have occurred — especially in their own families. They need to do this, however, in order to recover from the negative effects of addiction.

We wrote this book to provide a vehicle for kids and parents (or counselors) to talk about these problems. Younger children will need an adult to read it to them, but older kids may want to read it themselves. It can also be colored, drawn, or written in to aid in a child's self-expression.

For any age group, it's important that the book serves to stimulate discussion. Kids need to talk about what's happened and how they feel about it.

The more kids understand this disease, and how it affects individuals and families, the better they will be able to handle the problems it has caused in their lives.

This book deals with both alcoholism and addiction to other drugs. We show families in which the mother is the addict; in others, it's the father. Addiction can involve either parent and affects people of all ages, ethnic backgrounds, occupations, religions, and income groups. We try to reflect this as we explore the broad range of experiences a child may have had.

What we've tried to show, most of all, is how kids *feel* about living with an addicted parent. We also talk about recovery — what it means, how people can change, and how important it is for parents and children to come to terms with how their lives will be different. . .free of dependency on alcohol or other drugs.

If you are a recovering parent, helping a child may remind you of past behaviors that you'd prefer to forget. Be patient. In the long run, everyone benefits when these important feelings and experiences are shared honestly in an atmosphere of caring and acceptance.

ABOUT THE PEOPLE WHO CREATED THIS BOOK

The people who created this book bring a lot of experience to this project. The writers have worked with kids and their families for many years. Janet Sinberg and Dennis Daley have written many books about all kinds of problems — about addiction, and about helping kids and families. The illustrator, Tim Hartman, is also an actor who has helped kids understand more about chemical dependency. They tell us:

Janet Sinberg

"One of the things I've learned from kids is that when they talk about their problems they feel better about themselves. I've also learned how important it is for them to find ways to talk with their parents — and for their parents to listen. I think books like this can help. I helped write it because I believe kids really matter and what they feel is very important."

Dennis Daley

"I've worked with addicts and their families for many years. I decided to do this kind of work because one of my parents is an alcoholic, and I wanted to help people who have this disease. I can remember many of the feelings I had when I was a kid — anger, sadness, anxiety, and disappointment. I wanted to share some of the things I know about addiction with you, while you're still a kid, so you can feel better about yourself now."

Tim Hartman

"Several years ago, I traveled around the country doing plays for kids about alcoholism and addiction to other drugs. I was surprised to see there were so many kids that had problems because their parents were chemically dependent. When I was asked to illustrate this book, I was excited because it gave me another way to help kids understand this problem."

I Can Talk about What Hurts

ABOUT ADDICTION

Some people have a sickness or disease called *addiction*. This means that they can't control some of their behavior like gambling or using drugs even though it has started to hurt them. People who are addicted to drugs are called *drug addicts*. If the drug they use is alcohol, they are called *alcoholics*.

Alcohol and other drugs are *chemicals* that alcoholics and drug addicts *depend* on just to feel normal. That's why their disease is called *chemical dependency*.

This book is about chemical dependency, and it's important to know that this kind of addiction is a disease. People don't have chemical dependency because they're bad or want to. It's caused by the way alcohol and other drugs affect addicts' bodies and how they think and feel.

While addiction is a terrible sickness, it's also important to know that people can get better. This is called *recovery*. There are all kinds of ways that people can get help to stop using alcohol or other drugs and feel good again.

We've worked with lots of kids whose families have all kinds of problems. Many of them have lived with a parent who drinks too much or uses other drugs. One of the things we've learned is that chemical dependency can hurt everyone in the family, even the people who aren't addicts!

Because chemical dependency can be pretty confusing and can cause so many problems, we wrote this book to help kids like you understand more about it. We're going to tell you some things about alcohol and other drugs and how addiction to them hurts parents and kids.

And, we'll tell you how lots of kids we know think and feel when a parent has this disease. You may feel some of the same things. There are ways that kids can make themselves feel better about this problem. One way is to talk about their feelings and some of the things that have happened to them.

Some parts of this book might remind you of something that's happened to you. And, that might make you feel pretty strange — even scared. If this happens, it's important for you to talk about your thoughts and feelings with your mom or dad, a counselor, or someone else you trust.

Most of all, we hope this book helps you. Remember, just as addicts can get better and be recovering from their disease, you can get over some of the problems that your parent's addiction has caused in your life.

ABOUT ALCOHOL

Lots of people drink alcoholic drinks like beer, wine, and liquor.

Most of these people don't become alcoholics. But some do, and they drink too much or too often. When they start drinking, they just can't stop and often get drunk.

That may sound pretty weird. When your mom or dad tells you to stop doing something, you can usually stop. Like if you're watching too much TV. . .or picking on your brother or sister. . .or eating too much candy.

Addiction to alcohol, or alcoholism, is different from those behaviors because it *controls* the people who suffer from it. Even when they know that drinking is bad for them, they just can't stop. Their bodies and minds won't let them stop, and they keep getting worse unless they get help.

That's what makes it a sickness or a disease.

ABOUT OTHER DRUGS

Other drugs can be pretty confusing. That's because there are so many kinds. Some drugs are useful and help people feel better when they are sick. These drugs are called *medicine*.

If you get sick with a cold or the flu, your mom or dad might give you aspirin or cough medicine. Or, you may have to go to the doctor to get other kinds of medicine to help you feel better. Sometimes you get it in a shot or with a prescription from the drug store.

When parents get sick, sometimes they also go to the doctor and may have to take medicine. But, just like an alcoholic drinking alcohol, if they continue to take too much of some kinds of drugs that are used for medicine, they become addicted. When this happens, their bodies and minds won't let them stop, even when they aren't sick anymore.

People usually start taking these drugs to help stop the pain of a sickness. Those who become addicted keep taking the drugs for the good feelings they seem to cause, even after the original pain is gone. Now they have a new sickness — chemical dependency. And, as their addiction gets worse, they *have* to take these drugs just to feel like they can get by.

Now, this is where it can really get confusing. There are a bunch of other drugs that people take to make them feel different that aren't even medicine!

People who become addicted start out taking these drugs to change their mood from normal or unhappy to what seems to be a better mood with more fun or pleasant feelings. This is called *getting high*. And, while people are high, they often believe that all their bad feelings and problems go away. This is one reason why addicts keep taking drugs. But as their disease progresses, or gets worse, they lose control over the drug and their feelings. Their bodies and minds need the drugs just to keep from feeling bad.

These drugs are taken all kinds of ways. Some come as pills that are swallowed. Others are taken as a shot with a needle. Some are smoked. And some are even sniffed up the nose.

You've probably heard about a lot of these drugs at school, on the news, or you've seen things about them on TV. They have different effects on people and have different names like cocaine, crack, marijuana or pot, speed, heroin, and so on.

Besides being addictive and dangerous, these drugs are also illegal. It's against the law to use them, sell them, or even have them around.

There is nothing good about these drugs. They only hurt, and sometimes even kill people.

HOW ADDICTION HURTS

When parents are addicted they may get sick a lot, miss work, or even lose their jobs. They may stay away from home too much. They are likely to have more accidents, like wrecking the car or falling or hurting themselves. Some may get into serious trouble with the law.

When people drink too much alcohol or use other drugs and are drunk or high, anything is possible. They may act really weird and not even seem like themselves. They can be nice one minute, and mean the next.

They often do things they wouldn't do if they weren't drunk or high...like telling lies or hurting other people.

That's because alcohol or other drugs control them. These chemicals affect the brain and can even give people crazy thoughts, or make them act really strange.

Sometimes, an addicted mom or dad can seem like two different people!

Some parents spend too much of their money on alcohol or other drugs. Then their kids may not get enough of what they need to be healthy and happy, like food, clothes, or just fun stuff like toys or going to the movies.

Other people in the family may lie or cover up for the addict. They pretend there isn't a problem, when there really is. Sometimes, they take over for the addict and do their jobs or chores at home.

In some families where there's chemical dependency, people have trouble getting along with each other. They get upset and angry and fight a lot of the time about all kinds of things. It's hard for them to show they love each other. They don't say enough nice things or hug or kiss enough to show that they care.

These families don't spend enough time or do fun things together. They may not go places as a family — like visiting people, or going to the movies or a park.

Chemical dependency can mess up special times like Christmas, other holidays, birthdays, or vacations. This makes kids feel disappointed and mad. It can make them wish they lived with a different family or had another mom or dad.

Sometimes the problems get so bad that parents get separated or divorced.

HOW KIDS FEEL ABOUT ALL OF THIS

We've talked to a lot of kids whose parents are alcoholics or are addicted to other drugs. They've told us what it's like for them and how they feel.

They've talked to us about spending a lot of their time feeling worried and scared. Some of them have gotten hurt or seen other people in their family get hurt by the alcoholic.

They've talked and talked about all kinds of things, and do you know what happened? When these kids started to share all the tough and confusing things that went on in their families, they started to feel better! They said it was just too hard to keep all their feelings inside.

When we told these kids we were writing a book about these kinds of problems, they thought it was a great idea! They asked us to tell you about some of the things that happened to them and how they felt about it. Maybe one of your parents is drinking too much or using other drugs. Or maybe they've stopped and these are things that used to happen. Either way, it might make you feel better to know you aren't the only one who has gone through something like this.

This is what they told us. . . .

"There's too much yelling and fighting in my house. Mom yells at Dad when he starts drinking. When Dad gets drunk, he fights with everybody. Mom, me, or my sister. Anybody.

"The weird thing is when he's not drinking, he can be really nice...even fun to be with. You know, sometimes it's kind of like two different people in the same body.

"It gets even worse when he starts hitting or breaking things. When he gets really drunk, if we say anything to him, we might get hit. It's happened to me and Mom. I get scared because my sister's so little. I'm afraid he might really hurt her!

"Sometimes I try and fight back. That's scary 'cause Dad's so big, and a kid like me doesn't have a chance.

"The worst part is that I feel scared a lot of the time. It's really bad when Dad's drinking. But when he isn't, I also get scared 'cause I worry about what it's going to be like the next time he does."

"My Mom's always getting high on cocaine. Sometimes she goes off and doesn't come home for a long time. I don't know where she is or when she's coming home. I really worry 'cause I think something bad happened to her. Other times she just falls asleep and I can't get her to wake up no matter what I do.

"I also worry about me, and I'm afraid to be at home alone or to have her so drugged up. What would it be like if there were a fire or something really bad happened?

"When Mom takes drugs, I worry because there's nobody to keep me safe.

"Sometimes, she's okay and doesn't take drugs for a while. Then, she takes pretty good care of me.

"That's the Mom I like!"

"We never seem to have enough money. Dad spends it all on beer, and there isn't enough left to buy things for us. There have been times when we didn't even have enough food 'cause he wouldn't give Mom money to go to the store. That made me really mad!

"Or, like the time he forgot it was my birthday. He just forgot it! Mom made me a cake and he didn't even know it was my birthday. I got furious! I called him names and told him I wished he would just go away and never come back again."

"Mom's always making promises she never keeps. She doesn't remember half of what she says. Somebody told me this kind of forgetting is called 'blacking out.' Like, she promises to do something or take me some place or pick me up, and she forgets.

"Sometimes she promises to stop doing drugs, but then she takes them again. I don't think you should promise something if you're not going to do it."

"Lots of times I end up having to do everything for my sister and brother. Like when Mom's too drunk to even make dinner. Or, when she's so hung over, I have to get them ready for school all by myself. I feel good helping them, but I think that's too much for a kid to have to do.

"Sometimes, I think the reason she drinks so much is because of me or my brother and sister. When Mom's drunk she tells us we're bad kids. She says we make her feel crazy and that's why she drinks.

"I don't think it's true. But, I wish she wouldn't blame us for all her problems."

"I feel like I should be able to stop Dad from using drugs. I don't know how, but I spend lots of time thinking about it. I figured out it doesn't do any good to talk to him when he's high.

"Once I tried hiding the drugs, but he found them anyway."

"I don't like to bring friends over to my house. I'm always afraid of what might happen. Like, Dad might start drinking or already be drunk.

"I get embarrassed when Dad acts weird or yells at us in front of my friends.

"Sometimes, I hate being at home. Going to school or being with my friends lets me forget about it...for a while. My older brother is hardly ever home. He says it gets too crazy when Dad drinks."

"I feel sad lots of the time. I'm sad 'cause Mom has all these problems. Sometimes, when I go to bed, I cry until I go to sleep. I wish she would just come in my room and hold me and make me feel better."

"Sometimes I pretend there's nothing wrong with Dad. I sit and think about a different kind of father. One that spends time doing things with me. One that doesn't forget promises or is never mean. And we have lots of fun together."

"When people ask me about my family, I say things are okay. I want them to be okay so bad that I act like nothing's wrong. Besides, Mom doesn't want me telling other people about bad things that go on in our family. I guess it's our secret."

"My parents got divorced 'cause Dad was always drinking. Mom says I can't go see him 'cause he might be drunk again. I wish I could though. I wish he'd just stop."

HOW ADDICTS AND THEIR FAMILIES GET BETTER

With help, people can begin to recover from chemical dependency. This means they must stop using alcohol or other drugs completely. They must also begin to change the way they think and feel. This is called being in *recovery* or staying *sober*.

Sometimes getting help means going into a treatment center, which may be in a hospital. These are special places where people called counselors, along with doctors and others, help addicts get off and stay off alcohol or other drugs.

While there, people can't drink or do other drugs. They spend a lot of time talking about their addiction and how it's hurt them and their family. They not only talk with counselors, but also in groups with other addicts. They help each other understand their disease. They also start learning ways to stay sober after they go back home.

There are other programs that people can attend where they don't go into a treatment center. The addicted person can live at home and go to talk with counselors at an office or a hospital. He or she also usually goes to groups and talks with other addicts.

So, at first, parents may spend a lot of time away from home getting help. They need to do this to get better. If they don't get help and stay sober, things will probably get worse.

Even when people leave a treatment center, they need to stay in a recovery program and may keep seeing a counselor. Usually, once a week or more, they go to special meetings for people who are recovering.

AA and NA are two of the best known of these self-help groups. AA stands for Alcoholics Anonymous, and NA is Narcotics Anonymous. When people go to these meetings they don't have to tell their last names, and they don't tell anyone outside the group who the other members are. This is what *anonymous* means, and it helps people protect their privacy.

These meetings really help recovering addicts because everyone has had the same kind of problem — being addicted to alcohol or other drugs. It gives people a chance to talk and share what it's been like for them.

They also learn more about their disease. One really important thing they learn is that they're never completely cured. They can never drink alcohol or use other drugs again — even a little bit, or even once in a while. But they also learn that they can be *recovering* from addiction for the rest of their lives. They can do this by never using chemicals and by continuing to work on their new ways of thinking and acting.

But other people in the family besides the addict will probably also need help. If your mom is addicted, your dad will probably go to meetings and may see a counselor. If your father's the addict, your mom will also probably need help. Sometimes everyone in the family will go together. The counselor may just want to talk to the kids a few times.

Getting help is a chance for people to talk about what living with addiction has been like and how they feel. At first, it may feel strange, but all this talking can really help.

You may wonder how talking about stuff does any good. It helps people figure out some of the things that have happened that don't make sense or feel right. It's just too hard to keep everything inside. If you're really mad or hurt or scared about something, it helps to talk about it. This way you learn that your feelings are okay and that people still care about you.

There are even special meetings just for kids called Alatots. There's also the same kind of thing for teenagers called Alateen. At these meetings, kids can discuss their fears, problems, hopes, and other feelings about addiction. It's a way of helping themselves and other kids who are facing the same kinds of problems. These meetings are anonymous just like AA and NA.

Kids can also help themselves feel better when they talk with someone older who they know and trust. It might be someone else in the family like a grandparent, aunt, or uncle. Or it could be a teacher, coach, minister, priest, or rabbi.

If your addicted parent is in recovery, you also need to talk with him or her. Whether you're mad, scared, or sad — whatever you're feeling — your parent needs to know what it's been like for you living with him or her as an addict.

When kids talk about addiction and the problems it causes, they begin to feel better. They don't need to feel so afraid or mad anymore. They can stop worrying so much and blaming themselves for their parent's illness.

Not everybody's problems are the same. The most important thing is to talk about what it's been like for *you*. No matter what you think or feel, it's okay to talk about your feelings and what is bothering you. Sometimes that's hard to do, especially if you've learned not to talk about family problems to other people.

What's important is that you begin to feel safe and happy and not worry so much. You've been through a lot if you've been living with chemical dependency.

Recovery can help everyone. You, your mom, dad, brothers, or sisters.

Knowing that your parent is not a bad person but has a disease will help you understand some of what's been happening. You can then come to believe that no matter what your parent did or said, your mom or dad can still love you.

When families get help, good things usually begin to happen. People start feeling better about themselves and each other. They can talk more, be more comfortable, do things together, and just have fun. This is because they are now better able to show their love for each other.

Even though things can get better, sometimes there will still be problems and arguments. All families are like that, and things are never perfect for anyone.

It's hard work at times for alcoholics and drug addicts to stay sober. When they use alcohol or other drugs again, this is called a *relapse* or a *slip*. This can be very upsetting, but it doesn't have to mean that all the good things that have started to happen have to be lost. Addicts can begin recovery again, as long as they understand they can't drink or use other drugs. And they need to remember to do the things that helped them get sober before. Like going to AA or NA meetings and seeing a counselor. And, if the relapse is really bad, they can go back to a treatment center.

It's also important for all people in the family to remember that they deserve to feel better and may need help at times. They can keep talking to each other, go to meetings, see a counselor, or whatever needs to be done to take care of themselves.

With recovery, chances are that things will get better most of
the time.

The kids we know told us that.

We hope it does for you and your family too.

THINGS FOR KIDS TO REMEMBER

- Addiction is a disease that affects everyone in the family, even the people who don't drink or use other drugs.

- Because your parent is addicted, it doesn't mean it's your fault or there's anything wrong with you.

- Some people have a hard time staying sober. If this is true of your parent, don't give up hope. Your parent can still come back to recovery.

- When a chemically dependent parent and the other people in the family get help for the addiction, things usually get better for everyone. Even if the addict won't admit to being sick and get help, the rest of the family can decide they're worth it and begin their own recovery.

- Kids have lots of feelings about living with an addicted parent. You can help yourself by talking about these feelings and the things that bother you.

- Recovery takes time. Things won't get better all at once. It takes awhile for everyone — the addict and the people in the family. Keep working at it.

IMPORTANT WORDS USED IN THIS BOOK

ADDICT – A person who can't control some of his or her behaviors like taking drugs, drinking too much alcohol or gambling, even though these behaviors cause serious problems.

ADDICTION – The disease or illness that an addict has.

ALATOT AND ALATEEN – Groups for kids and teenagers who have someone important to them who is addicted to alcohol or other drugs. Here they can share what it's been like and how they feel about living with an addicted person.

ALCOHOL – The drug in beer, wine, and liquor.

ALCOHOLICS ANONYMOUS (AA) – Groups of alcoholics who meet to help each other not drink.

ALCOHOLISM – The disease of addiction to alcohol.

BLACK OUT – Memory loss about a certain period of time, caused by the use of too much alcohol or other drugs.

CHEMICAL DEPENDENCY – The disease of addiction to any drug, including alcohol.

CLEAN – A word used to describe a drug addict who has stopped using drugs.

COUNSELOR – A specially trained person who helps people talk about and understand their problems. A *chemical dependency counselor* works especially with addicts and sometimes their families.

DENIAL – Pretending that a problem doesn't exist.

DRUG – A chemical that is taken to change something in the body. Some drugs are helpful, like aspirin for a headache. Others, like cocaine, are very harmful.

DRUG ADDICT – A person who is addicted to drugs other than alcohol.

MOOD – A feeling that people have about themselves and their lives. *Altering a mood* means to change it.

NARCOTICS ANONYMOUS (NA) – Groups of drug addicts who meet to help each other not take drugs.

RECOVERY – Getting over the problems caused by addiction. For an *addict*, that means stopping addictive behavior — not using alcohol or other drugs. For *the people around an addict*, that means doing what's healthy for themselves instead of having their lives run by addictive behavior.

RELAPSE – When a person goes back to using alcohol or other drugs, after being in recovery for awhile.

SOBER – A word used to describe addicts who have stopped drinking.

TREATMENT – Counseling and group meetings working together to help addicts recover.

TWELVE STEPS – Twelve suggestions given in the book, *Alcoholics Anonymous*, which help alcoholics and addicts to other drugs to stop using them and to learn how to live clean and sober.

SOME NOTES FOR PARENTS

Some Important Things to Know About Addiction

Drug addiction, or chemical dependency, is a disease that tears at the very fabric of our society. All age, ethnic, occupational, religious, social, and income groups are affected. It is a cunning and baffling disease that absolutely defies logic. Addicted people continue to use chemicals because they have the disease. They don't need any other reason.

It is also a no-fault disease. It is not the result of willful misconduct, but comes from a combination of factors:

- *Biological* - differences in brain chemistry or the way the body reacts to chemicals.
- *Psychological* - personality, coping styles, and learned behaviors.
- *Social* - availability of chemicals, relationships, and the influence of peers or the community.
- *Spiritual* - meaning and connection with the world, especially relationships with other people.

As a disease, chemical dependency usually shows more in people's behavior than in their medical symptoms. Untreated, it can be fatal. Too many addicts die from medical problems, accidents, and suicide. Not only are the addicts' life spans likely to be shorter, far too many innocent victims die as the result of their accidents. The most common accidents are still the result of driving while intoxicated. Addicts also have a greater chance for family, psychological, work, school, legal, and spiritual problems.

It's a strange disease where one of the main symptoms is not knowing one has it. This is called *denial,* and it is the reason so many people never get help. They cannot see their own problem, and many have to be talked to, or forced into receiving help.

A person can be dependent even if chemicals aren't used every day, in large quantities, or always to the point of intoxication.

Although people become addicted to many different substances, the most common is still alcohol. An addict may show several or all of these signs: frequent intoxication, black outs, inability to cut down or stop, increased tolerance, withdrawal sickness, preoccupation, or continued use despite harmful consequences.

Often, family members try to live as normally as possible, though their situation is far from normal. They often deny or minimize the serious nature of the problem, which consumes much of their energy. Their lives are structured around the addict and his or her needs. It's not unusual to see them covering up for addicted family members, such as taking over their responsibilities or bailing them out of trouble. This is called *enabling.* Through what are meant as "helpful" actions, the addict is enabled to continue living with dependency. The real problem, addiction, is masked and, in the long run, things only get worse.

Chemical dependency often runs in families. Many have more than one member with an addiction, and addiction is commonly seen across several generations. Just as this disease affects the addict, there are negative consequences for the whole family. These may appear as physical or mental problems, difficulty in relationships, trouble at work or school, or problems in just about any other area of life.

It is important to note that not all families or individual members are negatively affected. While some may develop deep emotional scars, others survive unharmed. With most families, however, there is some degree of harm, depending on how long before the addict hits bottom, financial hardships, or extremes such as violent behavior — including emotional or sexual abuse.

Some Important Things to Know
About Children with Addicted Parents

When children are very young, they look to their parents for their basic security, for providing organization in their environment and their lives. As they grow older, they have other experiences in day care, school, peer relationships, with other relatives, religious groups, and sports teams that help to shape their attitudes and behaviors. Ideally, they learn to trust others and slowly become more independent. In small, gradual steps they move away from total dependency on the family until they establish their own identities in the world.

Children living with an addicted parent have often experienced a home and family that has been unpredictable. As a result, they may feel insecure and anxious, and they find it difficult to form successful relationships with others. In recent years, research studies have been conducted on *adult* children of alcoholics — those who, as children, were raised by chemically dependent parents. In many instances, researchers found that these children of alcoholics suffered profound effects in childhood that carried over into their adult personalities and behaviors.

Not all children are so adversely affected. Some develop coping mechanisms or healthy relationships that help to offset some of the negative effects. Most, however, are adversely affected to one degree or another. Just as an addict requires help in the recovery process, children also need help in overcoming the trauma of a parent's chemical dependency. With help, they're given a better chance to become emotionally stable adults who don't carry residual effects of their parents' problems.

Some kids:

- Worry about many things like the health of the addict, the welfare of the other parent, the fighting and arguing that so often occurs, and their own safety or that of siblings. Some worry more when they're away from home because they have fantasies about what's happening in their absence, and feel they are less in control.
- Feel anxious and afraid of the future. They are unsure of themselves and lack self-confidence.
- Believe they are to blame for a parent's drinking or other drug use. Many will take on the responsibility of trying to control or stop the addict's use.
- Feel confused, angry, or disappointed about broken promises or lack of attention. They may feel unwanted, unloved, and fear that no one will take care of them or that they'll be abandoned entirely.
- Keep their thoughts and feelings to themselves. They may be very upset and appear as though everything is fine. Others may show their feelings with attention-getting behavior and getting in all kinds of trouble.

Given all these possibilities, the remarkable thing about many children is their resilient nature and ability to survive and even transcend the most difficult situations.

About Recovery

Recovery from chemical dependency means learning to live without alcohol or other drugs, and making changes in oneself and lifestyle. Recovery is possible — no matter how bad the addiction is. It is an ongoing process that takes time and hard work. People stay in recovery programs for years; many remain for their entire lives.

Many professional programs and services are available to help addicted people and the families. Each case is different and must be evaluated on an individual basis. Some addicts require an inpatient program at a rehabilitation center or hospital, while others need outpatient counseling. Still others are able to begin recovery entirely through self-help groups. Twelve Step programs such as Alcoholics Anonymous (AA), and Narcotics Anonymous (NA), have proven extremely important for ongoing recovery.

Recovery for the family means becoming educated about the disease. It also requires change — stopping the denial or enabling behaviors, and learning new ones. When families become involved in recovery programs, things tend to go more smoothly for all concerned. Not everyone will need extensive treatment, but families will have to learn to talk about how chemical dependency has affected each member. Twelve Step programs such as Al-Anon and Nar-Anon are attended by family members concerned with their ongoing recovery.

Anyone in treatment, no matter how motivated, can relapse. But this doesn't have to mean that all is lost. Recovery is still possible, and many learn from relapse experiences, using them to strengthen future recovery efforts.

Recovering addicts and their families prove time and again that change is possible. The earlier children in recovering families are given the permission and tools for change, the more likely the devastating cycle of addiction will be interrupted so that they and their children are given a better chance to escape the tragedy of this disease.

We hope this book can be one of those tools for you and your kids.

HOW TO USE THIS BOOK:
A BRIEF LOOK AT TALKING TO KIDS ABOUT ADDICTION AND USING THIS BOOK FOR PARENTS AND TEACHERS

- Kids who live with an addicted parent often experience strong feelings even if they don't express themselves openly. You'll need to encourage and give your child permission to express his or her feelings, even (maybe especially) the ones that might make you feel uncomfortable — like anger or sadness. It's very important for them to get these feelings out in the open.

- Answer all their questions as honestly as you can.

- Try to help your child understand addiction and recovery, both the concepts and what these experiences mean in your life.

- If you are recovering, you don't have to defend yourself. Remember, addiction is a no-fault disease.

- If you are recovering, remember your children when you come to Steps Eight and Nine. If you are just starting recovery, you may want to ask your counselor or AA/NA sponsor to help you with these Steps.

- Avoid preaching.

- Remember, all the teaching and sharing you do will have little impact if you don't spend time with your child and show that you care.

RESOURCES FOR ADULTS

A variety of professional and self-help programs are available to help individuals who have chemical dependency problems, as well as their families. Professional services include assessment or evaluation, intervention, education, and inpatient or outpatient treatment. For more information, contact your local alcohol and drug abuse treatment clinic or your local mental health center.

Many different self-help programs are available as well. The most common ones include Alcoholics Anonymous (AA), Al-Anon, Narcotics Anonymous (NA), and Nar-Anon. You can contact your local AA or NA chapter for more information, or contact the national offices.

Al-Anon Family Group Headquarters, Inc.
PO Box 1821
Madison Square Station
New York, NY 10159

Alcoholics Anonymous World Services, Inc.
Box 459
Grand Central Station
New York, NY 10163

Narcotics Anonymous World Service Office, Inc.
PO Box 9999
Van Nuys, CA 91409

RESOURCES FOR KIDS

Services for children and teens are also available in many communities. More and more treatment clinics are offering special programs for kids to help them deal with the effects of a parent's addiction. You can contact your local alcohol and drug abuse treatment clinic to find out what is available in your community. Also, some schools offer educational and counseling services for kids who have alcohol or other drug problems, or who come from families where these problems exist. Contact your local school district for more information.

You can also contact your local chapter of Al-Anon and ask about Alateen meetings (for kids ages thirteen through eighteen) or Alatots (for younger kids). These programs are geared toward helping kids who have a parent with an addiction problem.

SUGGESTED READING

Ackerman, Robert. *Children of Alcoholics: A Guidebook for Educators, Therapists, and Parents,* 2d ed. Homes Beach, Fla: Learning Publications, 1982.

Alcoholics Anonymous (Big Book), 3d ed. New York: AA World Services, Inc., 1976.

Al-Anon's Twelve Steps and Twelve Traditions. New York: Al-Anon Family Groups, 1981.

Alateen: Hope for Children of Alcoholics. New York: Al-Anon Family Groups, 1981.

Black, Claudia. *My Dad Loves Me: My Dad Has a Disease.* Calif: ACT, 1979.

——. *It Will Never Happen to Me.* Denver: MAC, 1982.

Brooks, Cathleen. *The Secret Everyone Knows.* Center City, Minn.: Hazelden Educational Materials, 1981.

Chemical Dependency and Recovery are a Family Affair. Minneapolis: Johnson Institute, 1969.

Cork, Margaret. *The Forgotten Children.* Toronto: Addiction Research Foundation, 1969.

Daley, Dennis. *Family Recovery Workbook: For Families Affected by Chemical Dependency.* Bradenton, Fla: Human Services Institute, 1987.

——. *Surviving Addiction: A Guide for Alcoholics, Drug Addicts, and Their Families.* New York: Gardner Press, 1989.

Narcotics Anonymous. Van Nuys, Calif: NA World Service Office, Inc., 1983.

Seixas, Judith, and Youcha, Geraldine. *Children of Alcoholism: A Survivor's Manual.* New York: Crown Publishers, 1985.

Wegscheider-Cruse, Sharon. *Another Chance: Hope and Health for the Alcoholic Family.* Calif: Science and Behavior Books, 1981.

Woititz, Janet. *Adult Children of Alcoholics.* Hollywood, Fla: Health Communications, 1985.

Other titles that will interest you...

My House Is Different
>*by Kathe DiGiovanni*
>A children's storybook about a young boy discovering how to feel good about himself despite his father's alcoholism. 32 pp. Part of Hazelden's Early Steps Series.
Order No. 1387

If Drugs Are So Bad,
Why Do So Many People Use Them?
>*written by J. Gillespie*
>*illustrated by L. K. Hanson*
>Written for pre-teens to adolescents (9-14), this pamphlet explains addiction and discusses the devastating effects that addiction to alcohol, nicotine, or street drugs can have on young people. The author offers believable and realistic alternatives to drug use. (Also available in leaflet form.) 32 pp. Part of Hazelden's Compass Series.
Order No. 5530

Growing Up Again
Parenting Ourselves, Parenting Our Children
>*by Jean Illsley Clarke and Connie Dawson*
>As adult children of alcoholic or other dysfunctional families, the vital elements of structure and nurture may have been lacking in our lives. This thoughtful, non-judgmental parenting resource offers support for healing ourselves and passing the healing on to our children. 190 pp.
Order No. 5063

**For price and order information please call one of our
Telephone Representatives. Ask for a free catalog describing
more than 1,000 items available through
Hazelden Educational Materials**

HAZELDEN EDUCATIONAL MATERIALS

1-800-328-9000	**1-800-257-0070**	**1-612-257-4010**
(Toll Free. U.S. Only)	(Toll Free. MN Only)	(AK and Outside U.S.)

Pleasant Valley Road • P.O. Box 176 • Center City, MN 55012-0176